FREYJA

THE SENSUAL MYSTIC

Freyja - The Sensual Mystic

Copyright © Nichole Muir

Contents

Chapter 1: The Goddess Reborn

In the pantheon of gods and goddesses from ancient times, there is perhaps no figure as enigmatic and multifaceted as Freyja, the Norse goddess of love, fertility, war, and wealth. While other deities have distinct roles and characteristics, Freyja's domain spans both the realms of passionate love and fierce battle, making her an intricate blend of strength and sensuality. In this chapter, we delve into the depths of her history, her significance in ancient

Norse mythology, and the rebirth of her teachings in the modern era.

The Enigmatic Freyja

Freyja, often referred to as the 'Lady', is a central figure in the Norse pantheon. She is the daughter of the sea god Njord, and the twin sister of Freyr. While her brother is closely associated with fertility and prosperity, Freyja's attributes encompass both love and war. This unique combination of attributes gives her a dual nature, allowing her to be both a deity of peace and a fierce warrior.

The etymology of her name provides some insight into her nature. 'Freyja' translates roughly to 'Lady' or 'Mistress', and this title is indicative of her elevated status among the gods. She is revered, not just for her beauty, but for her wisdom and power.

In Norse mythology, Freyja is often depicted as a beautiful woman adorned with feathers, riding a chariot drawn by two magnificent cats. Her allure is undeniable, but her fierceness is equally apparent. She is the ruler of Fólkvangr, a meadow where half of those who die in combat go to spend their afterlife, while the other half is chosen by Odin for Valhalla. This shared responsibility between Odin, the all-father, and Freyja speaks volumes about her significance and stature in Norse beliefs.

Freyja's Multifaceted Roles

While love and fertility are her primary domains, Freyja's influence does not stop there. She is also revered as a patroness of seers and the practice of Seidr, an ancient form of Norse magic tied to fate and prophecy. This role emphasizes her connection with mysteries and the hidden aspects of existence.

Her relationship with the Brisingamen, her treasured necklace, further accentuates her complexity. The tales speak of her determination and the sacrifices she was willing to make to acquire this piece of jewelry, which was more than mere adornment. It symbolized her power and divine authority.

Perhaps, one of the most poignant aspects of Freyja's mythology is her eternal search for her lost husband, Óðr. Her tears, turned to gold and amber, speak of the profound sorrow and love she felt, underscoring her deeply emotional nature.

The Goddess in Modern Times

While the Viking Age and the prominence of Norse mythology have long passed, the resonance of Freyja's teachings remains. Today, in a world that often creates dichotomies between strength and vulnerability, war and peace, Freyja stands as a testament to the idea that these dualities can coexist harmoniously within a single entity.

The modern resurgence in pagan practices and the revival of ancient spiritual traditions have given Freyja a new lease on life. She is no longer just a figure of ancient tales but has become a symbol for those seeking balance in their lives.

In the realm of modern spirituality, Freyja's teachings on embracing both our gentle and fierce natures are more relevant than ever. She teaches us that love does not make us weak, and strength does not rob us of our capacity for deep emotion.

Contemporary followers of Norse paganism, often referred to as Heathens or Asatruar, have rekindled the practices and rituals associated with Freyja. This resurgence is not just a mere revival of old rituals but is a testament to the timeless nature of the wisdom that Freyja embodies.

The rise of feminist movements and the discourse on female empowerment have also found a symbol in Freyja. She embodies the ideal that femininity, in all its forms, is powerful. Whether as a lover, a mother, a warrior, or a seer, Freyja shows that every facet of femininity is filled with strength and significance.

Freyja, the Norse goddess of love, fertility, and war, offers a rich tapestry of stories, attributes, and lessons. From the ancient halls of Valhalla to the modern temples and sacred groves, her influence has been unwavering. In her, we find the intricate dance of duality - love and war, gentleness and fierceness, mystery and revelation.

As we delve deeper into her tales and teachings, it becomes evident that Freyja is not just a deity of the past. She is a goddess reborn, her wisdom echoing in the hearts of those who seek balance, empowerment, and the true essence of passion and strength.

The journey with Freyja has only just begun, and as we unravel her mysteries, we will find reflections of our own souls, our desires, and our dreams.

She beckons us to embrace all facets of ourselves, to find power in vulnerability, and to understand that in every ending, there is the promise of rebirth.

Chapter 2: Embracing the Dual Energies

When we look to the pantheon of gods and goddesses across different mythologies, few figures are as enigmatic and multifaceted as Freyja. At the heart of her mystique is the profound dual energy she embodies - that of the warrior and the lover. By understanding and integrating these energies, we can learn to lead richer, more harmonious lives.

The Fusion of Warrior and Lover in Freyja

The Norse tales are filled with gods of war, love, wisdom, and trickery. Yet, in the figure of Freyja, the seemingly opposing forces of war and love converge. Often, in mythologies worldwide, love deities are depicted as passive, delicate, and removed from the brutalities of war. But not Freyja. She is a passionate lover, an enchantress who can melt the coldest of hearts, and simultaneously, a fierce warrior, riding into battles and leading the valiant dead.

Freyja's residence, Fólkvangr, is a realm where half of those who die in combat go, while the other half is chosen by Odin for Valhalla. This speaks volumes about her standing and her warrior prowess. Unlike other love goddesses, she does not shy away from the battlefield. Instead, she claims her rightful place, choosing among the bravest of warriors and embracing them in her hall.

At the same time, Freyja's love stories and quests, especially her search for the precious Brisingamen necklace, exemplify her lover aspect. This necklace, a symbol of beauty and desire, underscores the lengths to which she would go to embrace her passions.

But why this unusual combination of the fierce warrior and passionate lover in one deity? It represents the primal energies of life itself. Life is an intricate dance of contrasts – day and night, birth and death, joy and sorrow. Freyja, in her dual nature, embodies the life force that accepts, integrates, and thrives amidst these polarities.

The Balance of Strength and Sensuality in Our Lives

There is a deep lesson for all of us in Freyja's duality. Society often encourages us to compartmentalize our emotions and traits. We are told to be strong, not to show weakness, and to separate our passions from our pragmatism. Freyja's life force challenges this. She shows us that strength does not stand in opposition to sensuality; instead, they enhance each other.

Imagine a world where we didn't feel the need to repress any aspect of ourselves. A world where our sensuality was seen as a form of strength and where our warrior spirit was not devoid of love and passion.

This balance has real-world implications. Think of the times when you faced challenges. Was it purely your determination that saw you through, or was it also the love and passion you had for your goal? When we're driven by passion, our challenges transform. They become not just battles to be won, but also dances to be enjoyed.

Moreover, embracing both strength and sensuality aids in forming deeper connections with others. When we show our vulnerabilities while also standing in our power, we create authentic relationships. We communicate that we can fight for and with our loved ones, and equally, be tender and compassionate.

Practical Steps to Embrace Dual Energies

To embrace Freyja's dual energies, we must start by acknowledging both within us. Here's how:

Self-reflection: Dedicate quiet moments to introspect. Ask yourself, when did you last allow your sensual side to express? When did you let your warrior spirit guide you? Jot down these moments and reflect.

Integrate in Daily Rituals: Begin your day with a mantra that honors both energies. Something like, "Today, I embrace my strength and my passions with equal fervor."

Physical Expression: Physical activity, like martial arts or dance, can be an excellent way to merge strength and sensuality. They teach discipline, focus, and grace.

Connect with Nature: Nature effortlessly balances contrasts – the fierce roar of the ocean and its serene beauty, the sturdy mountains and the gentle sway of meadows. Spending time in nature can be therapeutic in finding your balance.

Seek Inspirations: Read stories or watch movies that showcase characters balancing their warrior and lover aspects. They can serve as reminders and guides.

Meditation and Visualization: Visualize a place where your warrior and lover energies merge, maybe a serene battlefield or a dance floor in the midst of a fortress. Regularly visiting this place in your mind can help solidify your understanding and integration of these energies.

In Freyja's duality, we find an ancient wisdom that is ever relevant. A wisdom that tells us that life's richness does not come from choosing between contrasts but from embracing them. By integrating our warrior and lover energies, just like Freyja, we can lead lives of passion and purpose, filled with strength and grace. Embracing this duality is not just about paying homage to an ancient goddess but about understanding the intricate tapestry of life and our place within it.

Chapter 3: The Sacred Feline - Symbols and Meanings

The feline species, revered for its grace, agility, and mysterious demeanor, has long held a place of prominence in various mythologies and spiritual practices around the world. In Norse mythology, and particularly in the tales of the goddess Freyja, the cat assumes an especially significant role. To truly understand Freyja's essence and teachings, one must delve into her association with these enigmatic creatures.

Freyja's Feline Chariot

Freyja, often depicted as the goddess of love, fertility, and sensuality, is also known for her warrior spirit. She embodies duality - a balance of softness and strength. This duality is beautifully reflected in her chosen mode of transportation: a chariot drawn by two large, majestic cats. Unlike the fiery steeds of other deities, Freyja's choice is at once unique and telling.

The imagery of a powerful goddess being pulled by cats rather than horses offers rich symbolic resonance. Cats, unlike horses, are notoriously independent creatures. They cannot be tamed or controlled with ease. Their decision to pull Freyja's chariot is not born out of subservience but out of mutual respect and affection. This relationship underscores Freyja's inherent respect for autonomy and her understanding of the need for consent and collaboration.

Furthermore, the cat's agile, silent movement speaks of subtlety and grace. In choosing them as her companions, Freyja emphasizes the virtues of stealth, patience, and calculated action. There's a lesson here about the quiet power of femininity, about the strength that lies not just in overt displays but in soft, subtle maneuvers.

The Cat in Spiritual Symbolism

The cat's role in spiritual and mythological narratives extends beyond Norse traditions. Often, they're seen as guardians of the spiritual realm. Their penetrating gaze seems to look beyond the mundane, suggesting a deeper insight into the unknown.

In ancient Egypt, the cat was revered and often associated with the goddess Bastet, a deity of home, fertility, and protection. Bastet, like Freyja, was often depicted with lioness features, emphasizing the feline's dual nature of nurturing mother and fierce protector.

This duality is evident in the cat's everyday behavior. They can be affectionate, seeking warmth and attention, but can swiftly transition into skilled hunters, attuned to their primal instincts. This switch between tenderness and assertiveness is a hallmark of the sacred feminine, and by extension, it encapsulates the essence of Freyja.

Cats and Sensuality

Observing a cat is a lesson in sensuality. Every movement they make, whether it's the gentle arching of their back, the languid stretch of their limbs, or the soft purring sound they emit, is a testament to being present in one's body and senses.

Cats teach us the importance of touch. They often seek physical contact, nudging their heads against us, or curling up in our laps, reminding us of the healing power of touch and closeness. In many ways, they embody the sensual energy that Freyja represents. Their comfort with their bodies, their evident enjoyment of simple pleasures like a sunbeam or a soft blanket, encourages us to embrace our own physicality, to cherish our senses, and to find joy in the simple, tactile experiences of life.

Moreover, their grooming rituals, the care with which they maintain their coats and cleanliness, speaks of self-love and self-care. They do not rush; they savor. In their deliberate, almost meditative grooming, we are reminded to care for ourselves, to honor our bodies, and to engage with the world in a manner that is both conscious and conscientious.

Reflections

Freyja's association with cats is not a mere quirk of mythology. It is a deliberate and profound symbol of her teachings. In the graceful feline, we see reflections of her dual nature - the nurturer and the warrior. We are reminded of the need for autonomy, the importance of mutual respect in relationships, and the power that lies in subtlety and softness.

In understanding the cat's role in spirituality and its embodiment of sensuality, we also gain insight into our own nature. We are, like the cat, beings of duality. We have the capacity for tenderness and strength, for introspection and action. Through the symbol of the feline, Freyja invites us to explore and embrace these facets of ourselves, to move through the world with grace, intention, and a profound sense of presence.

In the tales of her cat-drawn chariot and in the deeper symbolism of the feline spirit, Freyja offers a path of understanding. She nudges us to question, to reflect, and ultimately, to embrace the multifaceted, mysterious, and deeply sensual beings that we truly are. The journey with Freyja is one of discovery, and in the soft purr of a cat or the quiet power of its gaze, we find echoes of her teachings, urging us onward, deeper into the realms of understanding and self-acceptance.

Chapter 4: Seidr – The Magic of Freyja

The enigmatic charm of Norse mythology has always revolved not just around its heroic sagas, but also its profound mysticism. Among the myriad magical practices, 'Seidr' stands out as a beacon, symbolizing the confluence of divination, alteration of fate, and profound connection to the unseen worlds. As the mistress of this magic, Freyja guides us through its realms, offering insights and powers that resonate beyond mere incantations.

The Roots of Seidr

Seidr, often translated as 'cord', 'string', or 'cordage', is a form of magic that primarily deals with the altering of reality and discerning the future. It's a sorcery that thrums with the primal forces of the universe. Rooted deeply in the ancient Norse traditions, it has been depicted in numerous sagas and eddas as the magic of transformation and prophecy.

It was said that those who practiced Seidr could connect with the cosmic weave of Norns, the goddesses of fate, thereby gaining insights into destiny and sometimes even altering its course. These practitioners were often called völvas or seiðkona (female) and seiðmaðr (male), though the majority of practitioners were women.

Freyja: The First Völva

In the vast pantheon of Norse deities, Freyja holds a special place as the first practitioner of Seidr. In the Ynglinga Saga, it's mentioned that she introduced this art to the Aesir gods, teaching even Odin, the chief of gods, its intricacies. While Odin's connection to Seidr is fascinating, and a testament to its power, it's in Freyja that the true essence of Seidr is epitomized.

Her dominion over love, beauty, fertility, and war gives her a unique position, which is further intensified by her profound skills in Seidr. As a deity, she embodies the Seidr's inherent duality: the ability to create and destroy, to love and war, to see the future and yet revel in the present.

The Rituals and Practices

Seidr was not just about spells and incantations; it was a ceremonial process. The ritual usually involved the seiðkona sitting on a high platform or a special seat, often referred to as the seiðhjallr or seiðstaðr. They would then enter a trance, induced by rhythmic drumming, chanting, and ritualistic songs called varðlokur. This trance allowed the practitioner to journey through the realms, connect with spirits, and gain insights.

Key elements in these ceremonies:

Staff: The seiðkona often carried a staff, symbolic of Yggdrasil, the cosmic World Tree. It was an instrument of power, guiding their journeys in the trance state.

Sacred Circle: Before beginning the ritual, a sacred circle was often drawn to protect the practitioner and the attendees from harmful spirits.

Songs and Chants: The varðlokur played a crucial role in guiding the seiðkona's consciousness. These chants were not just melodies; they were maps to the cosmos.

Seidr in Modern Spiritual Practice

For those seeking to incorporate Seidr into their spiritual practices today, it's essential to approach it with respect and understanding. This is not just a relic from the past but a living tradition for many.

Meditative Journeys: Start with guided meditations that resonate with the essence of Seidr. This can be a prelude to the deeper trance work characteristic of Seidr.

Nature Connection: Seidr thrives in connection with nature. Regularly spend time outdoors, especially in forests or near water bodies. Try to connect with the essence of nature, feeling its pulse, its rhythm, and its mysteries.

Study the Eddas and Sagas: Before delving deep, familiarize yourself with the primary sources. Read about the adventures of Freyja, the wisdom of Odin, and the tales of many völvas.

Seek Guidance: Like all profound spiritual practices, Seidr is best learned under guidance. Seek out practitioners or spiritual mentors who can guide you through its intricacies.

Seidr's Relevance Today

In a world that often seems disconnected from its roots, practices like Seidr remind us of the interconnectedness of all beings. The web of fate that the Norns weave isn't just a Norse concept but a universal one. In every decision, every choice, there's a ripple in the cosmic pond.

By understanding and, to an extent, mastering the art of Seidr, one aligns better with their purpose in this vast cosmic dance. Freyja, in her infinite wisdom and beauty, serves not just as a deity to be revered but also as a mentor. Through her, the power of love and war, past and future, life and death, can be understood and embraced.

Seidr is more than just an ancient art; it's a pathway to understanding the universe's deeper mysteries. With Freyja as a guiding star, this journey becomes not just insightful but transformative. In her magic, in her Seidr, lies the key to many of life's profound questions.

It's a magic that beckons, promising insights, transformation, and a deeper connection with the cosmic dance of existence.

Chapter 5: Embodying Sensuality

In the woven tapestry of life and mythology, few deities stand as prominently for sensuality as Freyja. The Norse goddess, draped in allure and draped in strength, beckons us to journey within, teaching us to embody and celebrate our inherent sensuality.

Freyja's Sensuality: A Symbol of Empowerment

The idea of sensuality has, for centuries, been tangled in a web of misunderstanding. In many traditions, it's been shunned, hidden away, or worse yet, misunderstood as mere physical attraction. Freyja, however, transcends such limited definitions. Her sensuality is not just about physicality, but also about embracing life with a passion, appreciating the textures of experiences, the flavors of moments, and the colors of emotions.

Embodying sensuality in the manner of Freyja means to see life as an exquisite tapestry of experiences. It's about grounding oneself in the present, feeling the weight of the world, the warmth of the sun, the caress of the breeze, and the rhythm of your own heartbeat.

Learning from Freyja: Sensuality as Spiritual Practice

Often, spirituality and sensuality are seen as opposing ends of a spectrum. Freyja defies this dichotomy. For her, sensuality is a spiritual act. When we appreciate the richness of life, the beauty around us, and the deep wells of emotion within us, we are in fact, connecting to the divine.

Every act can become a sensual ritual – be it the way we touch, the way we eat, the way we dance, or even the way we breathe. This is the wisdom of Freyja – to see every act, no matter how mundane, as a possibility for a deeper connection with the world and ourselves.

Practices to Embrace Sensuality:

Mindful Touch:

Begin by setting aside a quiet time for yourself. Sit or lie down comfortably, ensuring you won't be disturbed. Close your eyes and take a few deep breaths. Slowly, with immense awareness, run your fingertips over your arms, legs, and face. Feel the sensation of your skin, its warmth, its texture. This is not a massage, but a way to connect with and appreciate your body.

Sensual Eating:

Choose a piece of fruit or a delicacy you love. Instead of eating it hastily, savor it. Feel its texture, its temperature. Taste its sweetness, its bitterness, its sourness. Let every bite be an experience, an event. This practice helps you to be in the moment and truly appreciate the beauty of the world.

Dance Meditation:

Put on some soft music, something that stirs your soul. Let yourself move, not in choreographed steps, but in the flow of the moment. Let your body express what words cannot. Lose yourself in the rhythms, and in doing so, find yourself.

Nature Walks:

There's a world of sensation outside our doors. Walk barefoot on the grass. Feel the coolness of the earth, the tickle of the blades of grass. Listen to the rustling leaves, the chirping birds. Nature is a symphony of sensations waiting to be explored.

Scented Journeys:

Scent has a powerful way of evoking emotions. Invest in some essential oils or scented candles. Breathe in their aroma deeply. Let them transport you to places of calm, excitement, or nostalgia.

A Ritual to Honor Our Sensual Selves:

End the day with a ritual bath. This isn't just about hygiene, but about honoring and pampering your body.

Setting the mood: Begin by dimming the lights. Light some candles, preferably scented with lavender or rose. These scents calm the mind and stimulate the senses.

The bath: Add Epsom salts to warm water. These salts relax the muscles and draw out toxins. Add a few drops of essential oils like jasmine or sandalwood. As you soak in, visualize all stress and negativity seeping out of your body into the water.

Mindful Cleansing: Use a scrub or a loofah. Feel its texture against your skin. As you scrub, visualize sloughing off any residual negativity or stress.

Finishing touches: Once you're done, don't just dry off hastily. Apply lotion or body oil with mindfulness. Appreciate the softness and strength of your body.

Embracing sensuality isn't about hedonism, but about living life to its fullest. It's about making every moment count, every experience valuable. Freyja's lessons on sensuality teach us that by being in touch with our senses, we connect with the essence of life itself.

The practices and exercises provided here are just a starting point.

As you progress, you'll discover your own ways to awaken and honor your sensual self, guided by the wisdom and energy of Freyja.

In doing so, remember that sensuality is not about pleasing others, but about understanding, appreciating, and celebrating oneself.

Let the journey with Freyja transform you. Embody sensuality, embrace life, and experience the magic that ensues.

Chapter 6: The Power of Desire

In every crevice of the human heart, there lies an ember. This ember, when nurtured, bursts forth as desire—a force so potent, it has shaped destinies, kindled revolutions, and spurred countless tales of love, ambition, and quest. To delve into the nature of desire is to unlock one of the most profound mysteries of the human experience.

The Nature of Desire

At its core, desire is a powerful longing. It transcends mere want; it is a deep-seated yearning that drives us, propels us forward, often pushing us beyond our limits. The etymology of the word 'desire' originates from the Latin 'de-sidere', which translates to 'from the stars'. This celestial origin reminds us that our desires, like the stars, are vast, illuminating, and can guide our path in the vast expanse of life's journey.

Yet, like any force, desire, in its raw form, can be chaotic and destructive. When uncontrolled, it can lead to obsession, addiction, and unquenchable thirst that remains elusive of true fulfillment. However, when harnessed and channeled with intention, it can be a profound catalyst for growth, both spiritually and personally.

Freyja's Teachings on Desire

In Norse mythology, Freyja, the goddess of love, fertility, and war, embodies a multifaceted nature of desire. Through her tales and teachings, we can glean insights on how to navigate our own desires.

Freyja's relentless quest for her treasured necklace, the Brisingamen, is a testament to the lengths one might go driven by desire. But her tale isn't just about possession. It's about understanding the intrinsic value of what one yearns for and recognizing the sacrifices and choices made in its pursuit. Freyja teaches us that desire, in its essence, is not just about attainment but also about the journey and the wisdom gleaned along the way.

Another poignant lesson emerges from her role as a leader of the Valkyries, the choosers of the slain. Here, Freyja's desires pivot from the personal to the collective, from the physical to the ethereal. She selects half of those who die in battle to come to her hall, Sessrúmnir. This speaks to the nature of desire as a selective force, one that compels us to make choices that align with our higher selves and greater purpose.

Harnessing Desire for Growth

Introspection: The first step in harnessing desire is to look inward. Understand the root of your desires. Are they born from personal longing, societal pressures, or are they echoes of past experiences? By identifying the true source, we can begin to distinguish between fleeting wants and genuine desires that resonate with our soul.

Alignment with Higher Purpose: Every desire offers a lesson, an opportunity for alignment with our higher self. If a desire consistently tugs at your heart, it might be a beacon pointing towards a larger purpose. Instead of suppressing or judging it, explore its depths and see where it leads.

Balanced Pursuit: Freyja's multifaceted nature reminds us of the balance required in pursuing our desires. Passion and ambition, while necessary, should be coupled with wisdom and restraint. This equilibrium ensures our pursuits enrich us rather than deplete us.

Release Attachment to Outcomes: Often, our suffering arises not from unfulfilled desires but from our attachment to specific outcomes. Freyja's tales teach us to relish the journey as much as, if not more than, the destination. By releasing our fixation on specific results, we open ourselves to a myriad of possibilities and experiences.

Celebrate Desire: In many spiritual and philosophical traditions, desire is often viewed as a hindrance to enlightenment or inner peace. However, Freyja's embrace of her desires, both profound and playful, offers a refreshing perspective. Desire, when acknowledged and celebrated, can be a deep wellspring of creativity, motivation, and connection.

Desire as a Spiritual Catalyst

Our desires, in their purest form, are soul's whispers—gentle nudges pushing us towards our destiny.

When we frame our desires within a spiritual context, they transform from mere wants to profound quests for growth, understanding, and fulfillment.

Imagine desire as a flame. When left unchecked, it can consume everything in its path. But when tended, respected, and understood, it provides warmth, light, and guidance.

By tapping into the age-old wisdom of Freyja and the lessons she offers on desire, we can learn to dance with this flame, letting it illuminate our path, warm our spirits, and kindle our growth in the vast tapestry of life.

Desire is not merely a human impulse but a potent force that, when understood and harnessed, can be a powerful vehicle for spiritual and personal evolution.

By delving deep into its nature and learning from the timeless teachings of Freyja, we can embark on a journey of profound transformation, fueled by the very desires that make us inherently human.

Chapter 7: The Dream Weaver

In the intricate tapestry of Norse mythology, dreams occupy a space of enigma and revelation, and no deity is more associated with this realm than Freyja. Often referred to as the "Dream Weaver," Freyja's dominion over dreams is not merely about passive visions; it's a rich world where she actively spins, weaves, and influences the dreamer's journey. This chapter delves into her profound connection to dreams, the techniques she bestowed for recalling these nocturnal tales, understanding their symbols, and the potent magic they hold.

Freyja's Dream Realm

To truly comprehend Freyja's connection to dreams, we must first understand the Norse perspective on this nightly phenomenon. In the Viking age, dreams were believed to be messages from the gods, omens of the future, or reflections of one's inner desires and fears. They weren't just random images; they held purpose, meaning, and power.

Freyja's association with dreams stems from her being a multidimensional deity. As a goddess of love, war, and magic, she reigns over many spheres of existence, one of which is the dream realm. The dreams under her influence are often vivid, intense, and filled with symbols and narratives that require interpretation. They aren't mere wanderings of an idle mind but powerful visions that can offer guidance, warnings, or insights into one's destiny.

The Role of a Dream Deity

As a dream deity, Freyja does more than merely oversee this realm. She actively engages with it, weaving dreams for mortals, granting them visions, or sometimes sending messages through these nocturnal journeys. She might use dreams to convey messages, provide comfort, or even warn of impending dangers.

A renowned story in Norse sagas mentions a Viking warrior who was deeply in love but was to set sail for a long voyage. The night before his departure, he dreamt of Freyja, who handed him a locket. Upon waking, he found the very locket from his dream by his bedside. This locket, a gift from the goddess, protected him during his journeys, and he returned home safely to his beloved. This tale is but one of the many instances where Freyja intervened in the lives of mortals through dreams.

Techniques for Dream Recall

The potency of dreams lies in our ability to recall and interpret them. Many followers of Freyja employ rituals and techniques to strengthen their dream recall. Here are some inspired by Freyja's teachings:

Sacred Sleep Space: Ensure that the space where you sleep is clean, peaceful, and free from distractions. This creates an environment conducive to divine energies.

Intention Setting: Before drifting off to sleep, set a clear intention to remember your dreams. A simple affirmation like, "I will remember and understand my dream when I wake," can work wonders.

Dream Journal: Keeping a dream journal by your bedside can be instrumental. Upon waking, even if in the middle of the night, immediately jot down whatever you remember. Over time, this practice strengthens recall.

Liminal Wakefulness: The space between being awake and asleep, the liminal state, is powerful for dream recall. Upon waking, before you fully open your eyes or move, try to hold onto the fragments of your dreams.

Understanding Dream Symbols

Dreams under Freyja's influence often carry powerful symbols. However, interpreting these symbols requires an understanding that their meanings might vary from person to person. A raging storm could mean chaos for one but could symbolize a cleansing force for another. Here are some steps to interpret dream symbols:

Emotional Resonance: Focus on the emotion the symbol evoked. Often, the emotional response can guide the interpretation.

Personal Associations: Understand your personal relationship with the symbol. For example, if you've always found crows mysterious due to personal experiences, then seeing a crow in your dream might bear a different meaning for you than for another.

Context: The setting and narrative context in which a symbol appears are essential. A serpent in a garden might symbolize temptation, but the same serpent rising as a protector in a battle has a different implication.

Dream Magic with Freyja

Harnessing the power of dreams for magical workings is an ancient art. With Freyja as the guiding deity, dream magic can become an even more potent tool. Here are ways to tap into dream magic:

Dream Pouches: Create a small pouch filled with herbs associated with dreams, like mugwort or lavender. Place this under your pillow to enhance prophetic dreams.

Dream Incantations: Before sleep, recite incantations or prayers to Freyja, asking her to guide your dreams for a particular purpose, be it seeking answers, spiritual growth, or even healing.

Lucid Dreaming: With practice, one can achieve a state of lucid dreaming, where they're aware they're dreaming and can control or direct the dream's course. This state is especially potent for magical workings.

Dreams, in the world of Freyja, are not just nighttime fantasies. They are profound spiritual experiences that offer a window into our soul, our destiny, and the cosmos. By understanding and harnessing their power, we not only honor Freyja but also unlock a deeper dimension of our existence. As the Dream Weaver, Freyja invites us all to this realm, urging us to see beyond the veils of night and into the heart of the universe.

Chapter 8: Freyja's Feathers - Transformations and Journeys

In the vast tapestry of Norse mythology, one emblem stands out as emblematic of transformation and freedom – Freyja's falcon-feather cloak. This iconic symbol has a depth and mystique that transcends mere legend. To understand Freyja's feathers is to embark on a journey of self-discovery and metamorphosis, paralleling the goddess herself. Let's dive deeper into the heart of this symbol, its origins, and how it can guide us on our personal transformative journeys.

The Mythical Essence of the Falcon-feather Cloak

Every symbol has a story. And in Norse mythology, tales are not just mere entertainment but encapsulate profound truths about human nature and the universe.

Freyja, as we know, is a goddess of love, fertility, and beauty. Yet, she is also a fierce warrior, one whose spirit embodies the boundless skies. Her falcon-feather cloak, or 'falcon skin', is more than a garment; it's an artifact of immense power. When worn, it allowed Freyja – and anyone else who donned it – to transform into a falcon, soaring high above the world, bridging the realms of gods and mortals.

The choice of a falcon is deliberate. In many cultures, this bird is a symbol of focus, vision, and freedom. Its ability to hover and observe the world from a great height, only to dive down with precision when needed, aligns with the many facets of Freyja. She too hovers between the worlds of love and war, passion and power, physicality and spirituality.

In one renowned tale, Loki, the trickster god, borrows this cloak to rescue Idun and her apples of youth from the giant Thjazi. This story is rife with deeper meanings: the idea that transformations, even temporary, can lead to significant actions; that the tools of love and beauty (Freyja's cloak) can be used to restore life and vitality (Idun's apples).

Interpreting the Cloak: Symbols of Transformation

All of us, at some point in our lives, yearn to break free from our limitations, to transform. We have moments where we wish to soar above our problems, to gain a clearer, bird's-eye view of our lives. In this context, Freyja's cloak is not just a mythological item but a symbol of transcendence, perspective, and liberation.

The act of transformation is two-fold. First, it's external, changing form like Freyja into a falcon. But more importantly, it's internal: a shift in perception, attitude, and soul. In wearing the cloak, Freyja demonstrates that true power doesn't stem from what we show to the world but from the internal transitions we undergo.

For us, these 'cloaks' or catalysts of transformation are everywhere. They can be experiences that change our perspective, relationships that challenge and grow us, or personal revelations that redefine our essence. The key is to recognize these catalysts and embrace them, for they are our falcon-feather cloaks, waiting to lift us into new realms of understanding.

Embarking on Our Transformative Journeys

Taking a cue from Freyja, how do we embark on our transformative journeys? How do we find and wear our metaphorical falcon-feather cloaks?

Self-Reflection: Before transformation can occur, we need to understand our current state. Dive deep within and ask: What binds you? What keeps your spirit from soaring? Recognizing our chains is the first step to breaking them.

Seek Catalysts: Freyja had her cloak. What's yours? It could be a new hobby, a book, a mentor, or even a challenging situation. Embrace these, for they push you to evolve.

Embrace Change: Transformation isn't always easy. Shifting forms, beliefs, or perspectives often comes with resistance. But remember, the most profound changes often come from the most challenging situations.

Vision from Above: Just like the falcon, take moments to gain a higher perspective. Step back from the minutiae of daily life. Look at the broader picture, the interconnectedness of events, emotions, and decisions.

Trust the Journey: Not all transformations are instantaneous. Some are gradual, evolving with time. Trust the process. Trust that every experience, good or bad, contributes to your journey of metamorphosis.

Seek Guidance: While Freyja had the innate power to use the cloak, Loki needed guidance.

Similarly, don't hesitate to seek guidance when needed. Sometimes, an external perspective can illuminate the path of transformation.

Celebrate the Transformed Self: Once you've undergone a transformation, take a moment to acknowledge and celebrate it.

This not only boosts confidence but also motivates further growth.

Freyja's falcon-feather cloak serves as a reminder that transformation is within reach for all of us. It's a journey, often challenging, but always rewarding.

By understanding the symbolism of this magnificent artifact and its essence, we can find the inspiration to embark on our transformative odysseys, always striving, always evolving, always soaring.

Chapter 9: Sacred Spaces and Altars

Throughout history, humans have felt the innate need to connect with the divine. One of the most tangible ways to create this bridge between the human and the celestial is by establishing sacred spaces and altars. Within the Norse tradition, honoring Freyja with such spaces not only serves as a testament to our devotion but also facilitates a stronger bond with her energies. In this chapter, we delve deep into the creation, purpose, and power of sacred spaces and altars dedicated to Freyja.

The Essence of Sacred Spaces

A sacred space is not just a physical location; it is an embodiment of intention, energy, and connection. It acts as a portal to the spiritual realm and a sanctuary for meditation, magic, and reflection. By designating an area as 'sacred', you are setting it apart from the mundane and everyday chaos, allowing for a more profound connection with the divine energies of Freyja.

But what makes a space truly sacred? It is the energy, reverence, and intention you pour into it. It's the moments of quiet reflection, the whispered prayers, and the rhythmic chants that elevate it from a mere space to a sacred sanctuary.

The Significance of Altars

While sacred spaces offer a broad realm of connection, altars are more specific focal points within that realm. An altar acts as a nexus of spiritual energy. It is a platform that holds sacred objects, offerings, and symbols representing Freyja, aiding in rituals, spells, and meditative practices. The altar is a testament to Freyja's multifaceted nature – her sensuality, her warrior spirit, her connection to Seidr magic, and her role as a dream weaver.

Creating a Sacred Space for Freyja

Selecting the Location: Find a space in your home or outdoors that feels serene. It could be a quiet corner of your bedroom, a secluded spot in your garden, or even a dedicated room if available.

Cleansing the Area: Before sanctifying a space, it's essential to cleanse it of any negative or stagnant energies. Traditionally, Norse practitioners would use juniper or cedar smudge sticks. Light the stick and let it smudge, then walk around the area, letting the smoke purify the space.

Establishing Boundaries: This can be as simple as visualizing a circle of light around your sacred space or physically demarcating it using stones, crystals, or a circle of salt. This acts as a protective barrier, keeping out unwanted energies.

Infusing the Space with Freyja's Essence: Consider placing items that resonate with Freyja's energy. This could include cat figurines (representing her chariot pulled by cats), feathers (alluding to her falcon-feather cloak), or even images of the moon.

Setting Up Freyja's Altar

The Altar Table: Start with a clean, flat surface. This could be a wooden table, a stone slab, or even a cloth spread on the ground. The material isn't as crucial as the intention behind it.

Central Representation: In the center, place an image or statue of Freyja. This serves as the focal point and helps in directing your energy and intention towards her.

Symbols of Power: Add symbols connected with Freyja. A necklace or pendant can represent the Brisingamen, her cherished necklace. A bowl of water might symbolize her deep connection to emotions and intuition.

Offerings: Regular offerings keep the connection alive. Traditional offerings for Freyja include honey, mead, amber, or even sweet-smelling flowers like roses.

Candles and Incense: Fire connects us to the divine, and its gentle flicker can aid in meditation. Incense, especially those with sandalwood or rose notes, can elevate the energy of the altar.

Tools for Seidr Magic: If you practice or wish to delve into Seidr, keep a wand, staff, or runes on your altar.

Using the Sacred Space and Altar

Once your sacred space and altar are set up, they become centers of power and connection. Spend time daily or as often as you can, meditating, offering, or practicing magic. As you sit in your sacred space, visualize Freyja's energies enveloping you, guiding you, and empowering you. Use the altar as a platform for spells, divinations, or even to pen down dreams and reflections.

The more you engage with your sacred space and altar, the more potent they become. Over time, merely entering this space will evoke a deep sense of tranquility, connection, and empowerment.

Sacred spaces and altars are more than just physical setups; they are living, breathing entities that grow, evolve, and resonate with our spiritual journeys.

In honoring Freyja through these sanctified platforms, we don't just pay homage to the goddess; we invite her essence into our lives, making our journey on this realm richer, deeper, and more connected.

With Freyja's blessings and the power of sacred spaces, we find ourselves at the cusp of spiritual evolution, ready to embrace the mysteries of life with grace, courage, and wisdom.

Chapter 10: Meditation with Freyja - An Intimate Connection

Meditation is often considered a bridge that connects our mortal realm with the vast cosmic truths. As with many deities, understanding Freyja isn't just about reading ancient texts or studying her myths. It is about experiencing her, feeling her energy, and inviting her essence into our consciousness. Meditation serves as the perfect vessel for this intimate communion.

The Importance of Meditation in Understanding Freyja's Teachings

Meditation, at its core, is about connection. Whether we aim to connect with our inner selves, the world around us, or the divine energies of the universe, the act of meditation allows us to transcend the boundaries of our mundane existence and touch something profound. When it comes to understanding Freyja, meditation becomes an even more significant tool.

Freyja is a goddess of many complexities. She embodies both war and love, strength and sensuality, magic and mystery. Such dualities might seem contradictory on the surface, but they are harmonious facets of her being. To grasp this harmony, to truly understand the depth of her teachings, one needs to move beyond intellectual comprehension and into experiential knowing. And that's where meditation shines.

Meditation permits us to silence the outer noise and tune into the subtle frequencies where deities like Freyja communicate. By meditating on her essence, we get to experience her teachings rather than just learn them. We can feel her strength, her sensuality, her magic, and her mystery in a way that books or lectures can never convey.

Moreover, meditating with the intention of connecting with Freyja allows us to access parts of ourselves that resonate with her energies. She can help unveil our hidden strengths, untapped sensuality, and latent magical abilities. Thus, by understanding Freyja, we also come to understand and embrace deeper parts of ourselves.

Guided Meditations to Connect with Freyja's Energy

The following are two guided meditations designed to help you intimately connect with Freyja's multifaceted energy:

Meditation 1: Embracing Freyja's Sensual Energy

Preparation: Find a quiet space where you won't be disturbed. Dim the lights, perhaps light a candle, and sit or lie down in a comfortable position. If you wish, you can have a symbol or image of Freyja nearby.

Breathing and Centering: Close your eyes and begin by taking deep breaths. Inhale positivity and peace, exhale any tension or worries. Feel your body relax with each breath.

Visualization: Imagine a vast, beautiful garden bathed in twilight. This garden is Freyja's realm, a space where her sensual and loving energy thrives. As you walk through the garden, you notice flowers that glow with a soft light, trees with silver leaves whispering ancient secrets, and a gentle stream that sings a lullaby of ages past.

Meeting Freyja: Ahead, under a canopy of stars, you see a figure. It's Freyja, radiant and resplendent. As you approach her, you feel a warmth emanating from her being. She beckons you to come closer.

Embracing Her Energy: Freyja reaches out and touches your heart. Instantly, a surge of love, sensuality, and confidence flows through you. You feel an awakening of senses you never knew you had. She is sharing her essence with you, showing you the depth of sensuality and love that resides within you.

Integration: Take a moment to bask in this energy. Feel every nuance of this sensual awakening. Know that this energy is always within you, waiting to be tapped into.

Returning: Slowly, thank Freyja for this gift. Begin to walk back through the garden, carrying this newfound energy within you. As you reach the edge of the garden, start to become aware of your surroundings. Gently wiggle your fingers and toes, and when you feel ready, open your eyes.

Meditation 2: Tapping into Freyja's Warrior Spirit

Preparation: As before, find a serene spot, ensuring you're comfortable. If you have a talisman or symbol of Freyja's warrior aspect, you can keep it with you.

Breathing and Grounding: Close your eyes, inhale deeply, drawing in courage and strength. Exhale out fear and doubt. Feel a solid connection to the earth beneath you.

Visualization: Envision a vast battlefield, post-war. The ground is scarred, but there's a certain peace and stillness. This is where Freyja's warrior spirit shines – in the aftermath, where battles of life have been fought, and lessons have been learned.

Meeting the Warrior: In the distance, Freyja stands tall, donned in her warrior attire. Her presence is commanding yet comforting. You walk towards her, feeling an increase in your own inner strength with each step.

Receiving Her Strength: Freyja hands you a shield – a symbol of protection and resilience. As you hold it, you feel its energy merging with yours, fortifying your spirit, and bolstering your resolve.

Embracing the Warrior Within: Stand tall with Freyja. Feel the warrior within you rise. This is the part of you that can face challenges, that can protect, that can fight for what's right and just.

Parting: With gratitude, hand back the shield to Freyja. She smiles, reminding you that the warrior's strength is always with you, even without the shield. Slowly, the battlefield fades, and you start becoming aware of your surroundings. When you're ready, open your eyes.

Meditation isn't just about relaxation or mindfulness. When directed with intent, it's a powerful tool to commune with the divine. Freyja, with her myriad of teachings, is waiting to guide those who seek her. All you need to do is close your eyes, breathe, and let her in.

Chapter 11: Rituals of Love and Passion

The word "ritual" often conjures images of arcane rites and esoteric ceremonies performed to invoke divinities, mark significant life events, or channel specific energies. In the context of Freyja, the Norse goddess known for her deep connections to love, sensuality, and passion, rituals take on a personal, intimate meaning. To delve into the rituals of love and passion is to craft personal ceremonies that honor the lover aspect of Freyja and to weave sensuality and intimacy into the very fabric of our spiritual practices.

The Foundations of Freyja's Love Rituals

In Norse mythology, Freyja wasn't just the goddess of love; she was the embodiment of it. Her stories, her allure, and her passions didn't restrict love to mere physical connections but elevated it to a powerful force that shapes destinies. To understand the rituals associated with her, one must first appreciate the vastness and depth of the love she represents.

Freyja's love encompasses more than just romantic affection. It speaks of love for oneself, for nature, for the ethereal, and for the depth of human experiences. In crafting rituals dedicated to her, we recognize and honor the multifaceted nature of love.

Self-Love: The First Ritual

The ritual of self-love is the foundational step. In Norse tales, Freyja's self-assuredness and self-worth are evident. She knows her worth, and she celebrates it, a lesson she imparts to her followers. Before seeking to understand or love another, it's vital to turn inward.

Preparation:

Choose a quiet space, preferably during the evening when the energies of the day start to settle. Surround yourself with objects that resonate with you: crystals like rose quartz, mirrors, personal ornaments, or even writings.

Execution:

Sit comfortably. Begin by breathing deeply, allowing the breath to center you. Imagine Freyja's energy, warm and radiant, enveloping you. Say aloud or in your heart, "I honor the love within me, as vast and infinite as the cosmos." Spend a few minutes meditating on this affirmation, letting it sink into your core.

Ritual of Romantic Love

Honoring romantic love connects us not only with another soul but with the energies of the universe. Freyja's tales often revolve around her romantic adventures, which, while sometimes tumultuous, always hold lessons of the heart's resilience.

Preparation:

This ritual is best performed with a partner, although it can be done solo, sending energy to a partner or future partner. Prepare a space with candles (preferably red or pink), rose petals, and two pieces of paper.

Execution:

Both partners should sit facing each other. If you're alone, visualize your partner or desired partner. Write down on the paper what love means to you. Share these definitions with each other. Then, fold the papers and place them together in a safe box or envelope. By doing this, you're merging and honoring each other's perceptions of love. Close with a shared affirmation, like: "Our love is a beacon, ever radiant, ever true."

Sensual Connection with Nature

Freyja's love wasn't restricted to beings; she loved nature, the world, and its beauty. Recognizing the sensuality in nature is a profound way to deepen our connection with the goddess.

Preparation:

Choose a natural setting: a garden, a forest, or even a quiet park. Remove your shoes to connect with the Earth.

Execution:

Walk slowly, letting every step be a kiss to Mother Earth. Feel the textures—the softness of the grass, the ruggedness of the soil. Close your eyes and feel the wind as a lover's caress. As you reconnect with nature, silently or aloud, say: "With every touch, every breath, I honor the sensuality of the world, the love of Freyja."

Intimate Meditation

Combining sensuality and spirituality, this meditation fosters a deeper connection with oneself or with a partner.

Preparation:

Create a comfortable space, free of distractions. Play soft, ambient music if desired.

Execution:

For solo practice, lie down comfortably. For partnered practice, lie down facing each other. Begin by syncing your breaths. Allow your hands to touch your skin or your partner's, feeling the warmth, the pulse of life beneath. This isn't about arousal but about sensing the divine energy that Freyja imparts. Meditate on the sensation, the connection, the love that pulses with every heartbeat. Conclude by giving thanks to Freyja for her lessons in love and passion.

Rituals are pathways to deeper understanding and connection. By aligning with the energies of love, sensuality, and passion embodied by Freyja, we not only honor her but also elevate our own spiritual practices. The beauty of these rituals lies in their adaptability and personal touch. They are not set in stone but are living practices that evolve with our own understanding and experience of love. Through them, we don't just honor the lover aspect of Freyja; we embrace it, becoming conduits of the divine love she represents.

Chapter 12: The Brisingamen - Jewels of Power

In the vast tapestry of Norse myths, few objects dazzle the imagination as much as Freyja's treasured necklace, the Brisingamen. This glittering emblem of power and beauty, steeped in legend and mystery, is more than just a piece of adornment. It represents the essence of Freyja herself – her passions, her strengths, her desires, and her immense magical prowess.

The Legendary Tale of Brisingamen

Our tale begins with Freyja, the Goddess of Love and War, wandering through the realms, captivated by the world's beauty. During one of her travels, she stumbled upon the realm of four dwarves named Alfrigg, Dvalin, Berling, and Grer. These dwarves were master craftsmen, known throughout the Nine Realms for their unparalleled skill in forging wondrous artifacts.

In the dim light of their underground forge, a radiant glow captured Freyja's eyes. Laid before her was a necklace of unparalleled beauty, its gems shimmering with a fire that mirrored the Northern Lights. It was the Brisingamen, the pinnacle of the dwarves' craftsmanship.

Captivated by its splendor, Freyja yearned for it. She offered gold, silver, and precious stones, but the dwarves had no interest in wealth; they already possessed vast treasures. Instead, they desired the company of the enchanting goddess, asking for her favor and attention for four nights, one night for each dwarf.

Although tales differ in their narration of what transpired during those nights, it is agreed that Freyja, recognizing the worth of the Brisingamen and what it could symbolize for her and her followers, acquiesced to their request. At the end of the fourth night, the necklace was hers.

The Brisingamen was not merely an ornament. It amplified Freyja's powers, allowing her to traverse between realms and cast spells with heightened potency. Its aura resonated with her being, making it an inseparable part of her identity.

However, possessing such a jewel came at a price. Loki, the trickster god, envious of her acquisition, would scheme to steal it. This led to tales of deceit, transformation, and the ongoing clash between Freyja's allure and Loki's mischief. Yet, through every trial and tribulation, the Brisingamen remained with Freyja, a testament to its bond with its rightful owner.

Adornment as Power

Jewelry, across civilizations and eras, has always been more than mere decoration. The ancient Egyptians saw it as a mark of status and divine protection. The Celts viewed it as a symbol of kinship and tribal identity. In India, jewelry is believed to harness cosmic energies, providing the wearer with spiritual benefits.

Similarly, the Brisingamen was Freyja's talisman, amplifying her essence. When she wore it, she was not just donning a necklace; she was embracing her heightened powers, her intensified allure, and her reinforced spiritual essence. It became an extension of her being.

Jewelry as Talismans: The Personal Brisingamen

Drawing inspiration from Freyja and the Brisingamen, we can see our jewelry as more than just ornaments. They can be talismans, imbued with personal meaning and power.

Each piece of jewelry we wear carries a story, an intention, or a memory. The ring passed down from a grandmother might carry her strength and wisdom. A pendant bought during travels might hold the spirit of adventure and the memories of a journey. By recognizing and honoring these stories, we turn these pieces into our personal Brisingamen – talismans of power, identity, and intention.

To transform jewelry into a talisman:

Mindful Selection: When buying or accepting a piece, be conscious of your reasons. Is it a reminder of personal growth? A symbol of love from someone special? By defining its purpose and meaning, you give it power.

Cleansing and Charging: Just like crystals, jewelry can be cleansed. You can leave them under moonlight, smudge them with sage, or simply wash them in saltwater. After cleansing, hold them close and infuse them with your intention.

Wear with Intention: Whenever you wear your talisman, recall its significance. Feel its weight and texture, and let its story and intention guide your actions and thoughts for the day.

The tale of the Brisingamen is more than an intriguing story from Norse mythology. It's a reflection on the power of adornment, the value of desire, and the essence of personal identity. Like Freyja, we all have our Brisingamen, whether they're heirlooms, gifts, or self-acquisitions. By honoring them, understanding their significance, and wearing them with intention, we turn them into sources of strength, wisdom, and personal magic.

Chapter 13: The Warrior's Heart

In the lush tapestry of Norse mythology, Freyja stands out not only as a goddess of love and sensuality but also as a fierce and determined warrior. This dual aspect of her nature is perhaps what makes her so compelling and relatable to many of us. We all have battles to fight, whether they're external challenges or internal struggles. But how often do we embrace these battles as pathways to growth? How frequently do we recognize the warrior within us, ready to face adversity head-on? It's time to delve deep into the warrior's heart and understand the lessons Freyja offers in this realm.

The Dichotomy of Love and War

At first glance, love and war might seem diametrically opposed. How can one deity embody both? But if we contemplate deeper, it becomes evident that these two forces are simply two sides of the same coin. Love often requires courage, resilience, and a willingness to fight for what we cherish. Conversely, in war, there are moments of passion, loyalty, and deep connections that are reminiscent of profound love.

Freyja's warrior spirit does not negate her sensuality; instead, it complements it. It's a testament that one can be soft and strong simultaneously. A warrior's heart can beat with love, and the flames of passion can ignite the courage to battle.

Battles We Face

The term "battle" often conjures images of wars, clashing swords, and physical confrontations. While these are indeed forms of battles, in our modern lives, our wars are frequently more abstract. They can range from battling mental health issues, standing up against injustices, confronting personal fears, to overcoming professional hurdles.

Recognizing our battles is the first step to addressing them. It's easy to shy away from challenges, hoping they'll disappear or resolve on their own. But Freyja's warrior spirit teaches us that facing them head-on is often the way forward.

Embracing the Warrior Within

Just as Freyja wields her sword with grace and precision, we too have an inherent warrior spirit within us. It's that voice that urges us to stand up after a fall, the inner strength that tells us to push forward despite the odds. It's the resilience we display when life throws curveballs our way.

To embrace our inner warrior, we must first acknowledge its presence. It's essential to understand that being a warrior doesn't mean being devoid of emotions or vulnerabilities. Instead, it means recognizing those vulnerabilities and using them as a driving force.

Meditation, reflection, and even physical activities like martial arts or sports can help us connect with our inner warrior. They challenge our limits, demand focus, and instill a sense of discipline - qualities inherent in every warrior.

The Lessons from Freyja's Battles

Freyja, despite her divine stature, was not exempt from challenges. From her quests to reclaim the precious Brisingamen necklace to her endless search for her lost husband Óðr, she faced numerous battles. Yet, she always emerged wiser and stronger.

There's a profound lesson in Freyja's tales for all of us. Every challenge we face, no matter how insurmountable it seems, carries with it a lesson. The pain, the struggle, the moments of doubt - they all lead to growth. It might not be apparent immediately, but with time, the wisdom unveils itself.

Growth Through Adversity

It's a universal truth that our most significant growth often comes from our toughest challenges. Just as muscles need resistance to grow, our spirit, too, needs adversities to evolve. Freyja's warrior spirit invites us to view our battles not as hindrances but as catalysts for growth.

When faced with a challenge, instead of asking, "Why me?", we can shift our perspective to "What is this teaching me?". This change in mindset, though subtle, can make a world of difference in how we approach problems.

The Path Forward

As we move forward, armed with the lessons from Freyja's warrior spirit, it's essential to remember that every battle won't end in victory. There will be times of defeat, moments of despair. But that's the nature of war and, indeed, life.

What matters is not the outcome of the battle but the heart with which we fight it. Freyja's tales remind us that the journey often holds more wisdom than the destination. So, with a warrior's heart and a lover's passion, we march on, knowing that every challenge is just another step in our grand journey of growth.

In the end, embracing Freyja's warrior spirit is not about becoming invincible but about understanding that true strength lies in facing adversities with courage, love, and the unyielding belief that growth awaits on the other side.

Chapter 14: Nature's Embrace - Lessons from the Land

Freyja, often envisioned with her golden tears and majestic presence, is deeply intertwined with the rich tapestry of nature. Her connection to the land is an enduring legacy that transcends myths and beckons us to explore the intricate relationship between divinity, the natural world, and the human soul.

The Nature of Freyja

When we consider the vastness of Norse mythology, Freyja stands as a beacon of nature's inherent power. She is not merely an observer of the land but an intrinsic part of it. Her tears, said to be made of gold, are often seen as symbols of the land's fertility and wealth. When she cries, the earth absorbs her essence, signifying the union of divinity with the terrestrial.

Nature, in the realm of Freyja, isn't a mere backdrop but a dynamic entity with its own consciousness and spirit. The forests, mountains, rivers, and meadows are alive, echoing with the whispers of ancient tales and timeless wisdom.

Lessons from the Land

Life, Death, and Rebirth

The most fundamental lesson that nature imparts, under the watchful eyes of Freyja, is the cyclical nature of existence. Trees shed their leaves in autumn, only for them to return in spring. Flowers bloom, wither, and then pave the way for the next generation. In these patterns, we witness the rhythms of life, death, and rebirth.

For the followers of Freyja, understanding this cycle is paramount. It reminds us of the transient nature of our own lives, the need to embrace change, and the hope that rebirth offers. Nature isn't morose about endings, because every ending is but a prelude to a new beginning.

Harmony and Balance

Freyja's tales often speak of her adventures, desires, and conflicts, yet they always underline the importance of balance. Nature, too, thrives on equilibrium. Predators and prey, sunshine and rain, growth and decay – they all play vital roles in maintaining the delicate balance of the ecosystem.

By observing nature, we realize that excess in any form disrupts harmony. Whether it's the greed of over-harvesting, the chaos of rampant wildfires, or the stillness of a prolonged winter, nature teaches us the value of moderation and the essence of balance.

The Power of Adaptability

The land under Freyja's gaze is not static. It evolves, adapts, and finds ways to thrive under various circumstances. Think of the hardy plants of the arctic tundras or the deep-rooted trees of windswept cliffs. They tell tales of resilience and adaptability.

In our own lives, challenges and changes are inevitable. Engaging with nature helps us understand that adaptability isn't just about surviving but about thriving amidst adversity.

Engaging with Nature: A Path to the Self and the Divine

Nature Meditation

One of the profound ways to deepen our connection to both nature and Freyja is through meditation. Begin by finding a quiet spot in nature. It could be a sunlit clearing, a serene lakeside, or even a secluded part of your garden.

Close your eyes and take deep breaths. Let the sounds of nature guide your senses. The rustling leaves, the distant chirps, or the gentle caress of the breeze. With each inhalation, envision the energy of the land and Freyja entering you. With each exhalation, let go of your worries, anchoring yourself deeper into the embrace of the earth.

Nature's Offerings

Nature is replete with offerings if we only take a moment to notice. Fallen leaves, petals, stones, or even the morning dew. Collect them. Not as a hoarder but as someone who understands their significance.

These offerings can be used to create a personal altar dedicated to Freyja or can be incorporated into rituals and spells. They are symbols of nature's bounty and Freyja's blessings.

Walking the Sacred Path

To truly understand nature's lessons and Freyja's wisdom, consider walking the land. Not as a casual stroll but as a pilgrimage. With every step, be mindful of the earth beneath, the sky above, and the world around. Feel the heartbeat of the land, and in that rhythm, you'll find the echoes of Freyja's songs.

As you walk, let nature guide your introspections. Let the towering mountains inspire you to surmount challenges, the flowing rivers to move ahead with grace, and the vast meadows to embrace openness.

Nature, in all its grandeur and subtlety, holds lessons that are both timeless and pertinent. Freyja, as the embodiment of nature's spirit, bridges the gap between the divine and the mortal realms. By engaging with nature, by truly immersing ourselves in its wonders, we don't just foster a connection to the goddess but also embark on a journey of self-discovery.

For in the heart of nature, amidst the dance of shadows and light, we find reflections of our own souls and whispers of the divine. Freyja's realm is not distant; it's right here, waiting for us to notice, to learn, and to grow.

Chapter 15: Lunar Magic with Freyja

The dance of the moon across the night sky is one of the most mesmerizing sights nature offers. Its ethereal glow, its waxing and waning, and the rhythms it inspires in the world around us have been sources of wonder for millennia. But the moon is more than just a celestial body; it is a potent symbol of cycles, emotions, intuition, and sensuality.

Freyja, the Sensual Mystic, shares a profound connection with the moon. In the heart of Norse mythology, the luminance of the moon and the allure of Freyja converge, weaving tales of magic, mystery, and seduction. This chapter unveils the depths of lunar magic in tandem with Freyja's teachings, guiding you through practices and rituals that align with the different phases of the moon.

The Moon and Freyja: A Cosmic Dance

In many ways, Freyja's essence resonates with the different aspects of the moon. Both are symbols of the feminine divine, carrying energies of intuition, mystery, and sensuality. Just as the moon affects the tides, so does Freyja influence the ebb and flow of our desires, dreams, and passions.

Freyja, with her dual aspects of warrior and lover, mirrors the duality of the moon. The moon's waxing phase echoes Freyja's warrior aspect, a time of growth and gaining strength. Its waning phase, on the other hand, resonates with her lover side, a period of introspection, release, and rejuvenation.

The Waxing Moon: Invoking the Warrior

As the moon transitions from its new phase, gradually unveiling more of itself, it's a period of growth, aspiration, and energy. It's the optimal time to invoke Freyja's warrior spirit.

Ritual: Shield of Intentions

Preparation: Find a quiet space where you can see the waxing moon, preferably outdoors. You'll need a small shield-shaped piece of paper, a pen, and a small dish of water.

Casting the Circle: Begin by grounding yourself. Feel the energies of the earth below and the moon above converging within you.

Writing Intentions: On the shield paper, write down what you wish to achieve or gain strength in during this waxing phase.

Moonlit Blessing: Hold the shield up to the moonlight, allowing the lunar glow to bathe your intentions. As you do this, recite: "Freyja, Warrior of the Night, empower these intentions with your might."

Sealing: Place the shield paper in the dish of water. As the paper becomes saturated, envision your intentions being absorbed, becoming one with the essence of Freyja and the moon. Let it dry naturally under the moonlight.

The Full Moon: Sensuality at Its Peak

At the full moon, the lunar energies are at their most potent, making it a perfect time to celebrate Freyja's sensuality.

Ritual: Dance of Desires

Preparation: Dress in flowing garments. Adorn yourself with any jewelry or accessories that make you feel sensual.

Lunar Gaze: Begin by standing under the full moon, feeling its luminance envelop you. Close your eyes and take a deep breath, tuning into the heightened energies around.

Sensual Dance: Allow your body to move freely, letting the lunar energies and thoughts of Freyja guide each step, twirl, and sway. This isn't about structured dance but rather expressing your inner desires and sensuality.

Reflection: Once you've allowed your energy to flow fully, sit and reflect on any emotions or insights that arose during the dance.

The Waning Moon: Embracing the Lover's Embrace

The waning phase signifies a period of release, relaxation, and rejuvenation. Here, one can channel Freyja's lover aspect.

Ritual: Bath of Release

Preparation: Gather essential oils like rose or jasmine, Epsom salts, and moonstone crystals.

Lunar Water: Collect water in a bowl and let it sit under the waning moon for a few hours.

Sacred Bath: Fill your bathtub and add the lunar-charged water. Mix in Epsom salts, a few drops of essential oil, and place the moonstone crystals in the water.

Bath Meditation: As you soak, visualize any stresses, worries, or negativity flowing out of you, absorbed by the water. Feel the embrace of Freyja comforting and rejuvenating you.

The New Moon: Mysteries and Beginnings

The new moon, with its dark sky, is a period of introspection, aligning with the mysteries of life.

Ritual: Dreaming with Freyja

Preparation: Have a journal, a pen, and a white candle.

Sacred Space: In a dark room, light the candle. This will be the only light, symbolizing the new moon's darkness and the potential within.

Dream Intent: Think of a question or mystery you want insights into. Write it down in the journal.

Sleep Meditation: As you lay down to sleep, recite: "Freyja, in this moon's embrace, reveal the answers in dream's space."

Recording: Upon waking, jot down any dreams or feelings in the journal.

By aligning with the lunar phases and invoking the energies of Freyja, one can weave a tapestry of magic, sensuality, and insight. This connection allows for a deeper understanding of oneself and the universe, drawing strength from both the Sensual Mystic and the celestial dance of the moon.

Chapter 16: Secrets of the Valkyries

The Norse pantheon is a colorful tapestry of deities, creatures, and beings, each with their distinct roles and attributes. Among these, the Valkyries stand out as figures of power, beauty, and mystery. As handmaidens of Freyja, they occupy an integral space in the mythological realm, serving both the goddess and the greater narrative of life, death, and destiny.

The Valkyries: Ethereal Maidens of Battle

The word 'Valkyrie' is derived from Old Norse "valkyrja", meaning "chooser of the slain." These divine figures are often visualized as warrior maidens, armored and riding on winged horses, soaring over battlefields and choosing the brave who would die and those who would live. While their primary function appears to be connected to warfare and the afterlife, they symbolize much more than just bringers of death.

In the grand design of Norse cosmology, every being has a role to play, a duty to perform. The Valkyries stand as intermediaries between the mortal realm and the divine, representing the cycle of life, death, and rebirth. They ensure that the brave and honorable warriors are rewarded in the afterlife, while also representing fate's unpredictability.

Freyja's Connection: Leading the Valkyries

While Odin, the Allfather, is often closely linked with the Valkyries, as he would welcome the chosen warriors to Valhalla, it is Freyja who led these divine maidens. Freyja, as the goddess of love, fertility, and war, commands the first choice among the slain. It's an intricate balance of her nature—both as a lover and a warrior—that she shares with her Valkyries.

The presence of Freyja as their leader further amplifies the complexity of the Valkyries. They are not merely instruments of death but serve a greater purpose in the cosmic cycle. Just as Freyja embodies sensuality and strength, the Valkyries personify the balance between the harsh realities of life and the allure of what lies beyond.

Guiding Souls: The Path to the Afterlife

One of the most sacred roles of the Valkyries is to guide the souls of fallen warriors to their rightful place in the afterlife. Those deemed worthy are escorted to Valhalla, Odin's great hall, where they prepare for Ragnarök, the prophesied end-of-days battle. The rest are taken to Fólkvangr, Freyja's realm—a meadow where souls find peace and reflection.

This division is not a simple split between 'good' and 'bad' warriors. Instead, it represents the broader understanding of life, where death is not an end but a transformation. In guiding these souls, the Valkyries oversee this transformation, ensuring that the brave are honored and that every soul finds its rightful place in the grand cycle of existence.

Life, Death, and the Valkyrie Wisdom

The Valkyries' role in the Norse cosmos offers profound insights into life and death. Life, as represented by the battles the warriors fight, is unpredictable, challenging, and often brutal. Yet, it is also a proving ground—a place where honor, courage, and determination are tested.

Death, on the other hand, is not a cessation but a transition. The Valkyries teach us that every end is a new beginning. Every sunset promises a sunrise. By guiding souls through this passage, they emphasize the interconnectedness of all phases of existence.

Freyja's Valkyries, therefore, challenge the conventional perspective on death. Instead of fearing it, they encourage us to understand and embrace it as an essential part of the journey. It's a journey where the destination is not as crucial as the lessons learned, the bonds formed, and the honor earned.

Embracing the Valkyrie Spirit

In today's world, we may not have ethereal maidens guiding us post-battle, but the spirit of the Valkyries remains relevant. Their essence encourages us to face challenges head-on, to live with honor and courage, and to understand that every ending holds the promise of a new beginning.

By integrating the wisdom of the Valkyries into our lives, we can approach our personal battles, whether they be emotional, physical, or spiritual, with a renewed sense of purpose. We can find solace in the fact that, much like the warriors of old, we are watched over, and that our struggles, successes, and even failures have meaning in the grand tapestry of existence.

In understanding the Valkyries, we unearth secrets not just about these divine maidens but about the nature of life and death itself. They stand as reminders that life, with all its unpredictability, is worth fighting for, and that death, while inevitable, is merely a passage to another chapter of our journey.

In Freyja's embrace and under her leadership, the Valkyries continue to inspire, reminding us of the beauty in every phase of existence, the honor in every challenge faced, and the eternal nature of the soul's journey. As guardians of the fallen and guides of the soul, their secrets are a testament to the intricate dance of life and death, a dance we are all a part of.

Chapter 17: Freyja in Everyday Life

The allure of ancient deities often lies in their grand narratives, their presence in epic tales, and the rituals that surround them. But the true measure of a deity's relevance and power is gauged by their applicability in our everyday lives. Freyja, as the Sensual Mystic, is not merely confined to the annals of Norse mythology. Her teachings, when understood deeply, weave seamlessly into our daily routines, relationships, and reflections.

Integrating Freyja's Teachings into Daily Choices

The essence of Freyja's teachings lies in embracing both strength and sensuality. It's a celebration of the self in all its facets. Each day, we are presented with countless choices. From the way we dress to the food we consume, from our interactions with others to our solitary reflections - Freyja's presence can be infused in each of these decisions.

Imagine starting your day by selecting an outfit. Instead of choosing purely on functionality or what's readily available, pause. Think about an attire that makes you feel both strong and sensual. It might be the softness of a particular fabric against your skin, or the bold color that gives you confidence. Here, you're not dressing for anyone else but yourself, acknowledging both your power and your vulnerability.

Similarly, when it comes to food, we can embrace both nourishment and indulgence. It's about savoring flavors, being present in the moment of consumption, and choosing foods that make us feel vibrant and alive.

Building Relationships with Freyja's Wisdom

Freyja's domain isn't limited to personal growth alone. Her teachings extend to our relationships as well. When engaging with loved ones, friends, or even acquaintances, imagine embodying the dual energies of Freyja. Be the listener, the empath, the nurturer, but also stand firm in your beliefs, and uphold your boundaries.

In disagreements, rather than resorting to aggression or complete submission, find that middle ground – where you can be compassionate and yet assertive. When love and intimacy come into the frame, embrace them with openness, celebrating the sensual being that you are, without forgetting the strength that lies within you.

Daily Devotion and Reflection

One doesn't need elaborate rituals to connect with Freyja daily. Simple acts can serve as devotion and a means to strengthen your bond with the goddess.

Morning Affirmations: Begin your day with affirmations that channel Freyja's energies. Something as simple as, "Today, I embrace my strength and sensuality," can set the tone for the day.

Nature Walks: Given Freyja's connection with nature, a walk amidst natural surroundings can be a meditative experience. As you stroll, be observant. Feel the earth beneath your feet, the wind against your skin, and let these sensations remind you of Freyja's teachings.

Journaling: Set aside a few minutes each day to journal your experiences. Reflect on where you felt Freyja's presence or where you could have invoked her teachings. This not only strengthens your connection with the deity but also serves as a tool for self-awareness.

Nightly Reflection: Before sleep, revisit your day. Think of moments where you truly embodied Freyja's essence and moments you faltered. Use this reflection not as a tool for self-critique but as a guide for growth.

Tips for Daily Connection

To truly integrate Freyja into everyday life, consider these simple yet profound tips:

Create a Freyja Corner: Dedicate a small space in your home to Freyja. It could be adorned with symbols associated with her, like a cat figurine or a replica of the Brisingamen necklace. Every time you pass by this corner, let it serve as a gentle reminder of her teachings.

Incorporate Scents: Freyja, being a goddess of love and sensuality, can be invoked through the power of scents. Consider using essential oils like rose or amber, either as a perfume or in a diffuser, to create an atmosphere that resonates with her energy.

Dedicate Actions to Freyja: It could be as simple as dedicating your yoga session or even your daily workout to her. By mentally offering these actions to Freyja, you align yourself with her energies.

Read and Reflect: Keep a quote or a story about Freyja handy. Perhaps on a post-it note on your desk or as a bookmark. Every time you come across it, take a moment to read and reflect, connecting with her essence.

Incorporating Freyja in everyday life isn't about grand gestures but the seamless integration of her teachings into our daily choices, relationships, and moments of reflection.

By doing so, we don't just honor the deity but also enrich our lives, making each day a blend of strength, sensuality, and profound wisdom.

With Freyja as a guiding force, every ordinary moment can be transformed into something truly magical.

Chapter 18: Dance of the Mystic - Moving with Freyja

The ancient rhythms of the earth pulse through our veins, calling us to remember, to reconnect, and to reawaken. These are the rhythms that the goddess Freyja danced to, and through dance, she tapped into the very core of her mystical energy. Just as Freyja wove magic with her steps, so too can we connect with her divine power through the art of dance.

The Primordial Pulse of Dance

Dance is as ancient as humanity itself. From the earliest civilizations, dance has been a medium for storytelling, celebration, and communion with the divine. The fluidity of movement and rhythm speaks to the soul in a language that words often cannot capture. This innate connection between body, rhythm, and spirit was well-understood by the Norse, and Freyja, in her infinite wisdom, personified this connection.

Freyja's energy is fluid, ever-shifting, and ever-evolving, much like the graceful and unpredictable patterns of a dance. When we dance, especially with intention and focus, we are tapping into this same energy. We channel the primal forces of the earth, the passion of fire, the depth of water, and the freedom of air. Dancing becomes a ritual, a way to meld with the universe and the divine.

Dance as Devotion

To truly connect with Freyja's energies through dance, one must first approach it as a sacred act of devotion. This is not dance for entertainment or for the gaze of others, but for the self and the divine. It's a ritualistic practice where the dancer surrenders to the moment, letting go of inhibitions, fears, and the conscious mind.

Begin by creating a sacred space. This could be anywhere you feel connected—be it a secluded spot in nature, a quiet room in your home, or a space specially set aside for spiritual practices. Light candles, burn incense, or play soft, rhythmic music to set the mood.

Stand in the center of your space, feet shoulder-width apart. Close your eyes and take a deep breath, drawing it in from the soles of your feet to the crown of your head. As you exhale, visualize any tensions, anxieties, or inhibitions leaving your body. Repeat this breathing exercise a few times, each time sinking deeper into a relaxed state.

Now, picture Freyja before you. Feel her presence, her strength, her sensuality, and her mystique. Open yourself up to her energy. Ask her to guide you, to move through you.

Begin to move slowly. There's no specific pattern or steps to follow. Let your body be guided by intuition and feeling. As you sway, twirl, leap, or simply walk in rhythmic circles, imagine Freyja dancing alongside you, her energy mirroring and melding with yours.

Harnessing Freyja's Power Through Dance

As you deepen your connection with Freyja through dance, you can begin to use specific rituals to harness her power:

Dance of Desire: This dance focuses on manifesting one's desires. Holding a clear intention of what you want, use the dance to raise energy. As you move, visualize your desire coming to fruition, feeling the emotions as if it's already happened.

Dance of Transformation: This dance focuses on personal growth and transformation. Begin by visualizing a cocoon around you. As you dance, imagine breaking free from this cocoon, emerging as a transformed being, leaving behind old habits and welcoming new energies.

Dance of Healing: Dancing can be therapeutic. If there's an area in your life or body that needs healing, focus on that area as you dance. Visualize Freyja's energy enveloping the area, soothing, and healing it.

Dance of Gratitude: A joyful dance where every step is a thank you to the universe, to Freyja, and to oneself. It celebrates the beauty of life and acknowledges the blessings, big or small.

To end any of these dances, slow your movements gradually, finally coming to a standstill. Take a few deep breaths, grounding yourself. Thank Freyja for her guidance and energy.

The Dance of the Mystic is more than just movement; it's a communion. It's a bridge that connects our earthly existence with the ethereal, the mundane with the divine. Every step taken, every twirl, every leap is an ode to Freyja, a song of the soul that resonates with her energy.

Dancing in the footsteps of Freyja is to embrace freedom, passion, transformation, and the divine mysteries of life. Whether you're a seasoned dancer or someone with two left feet, the essence lies not in the perfection of steps but in the intention, the emotion, and the connection.

So, the next time you feel a pull, a rhythm calling out to you, remember Freyja and her mystic dance. Let your body move, let your spirit soar, and let the dance become a portal to the divine.

Chapter 19: Beyond Myths - The Living Freyja

In the vast corridors of Norse mythology, where gods and goddesses dance amidst a tapestry of heroic sagas, a figure stands out – Freyja. Often, we hear her tales recounted with an air of antiquity, something far removed from our present reality. She's portrayed with her lustrous golden necklace, the Brisingamen, astride her feline-driven chariot, or soaring the skies with her falcon-feathered cloak. But as we embark on this chapter, let's cast aside the myths for a moment and ask a daring question: What if Freyja, instead of being a mere figment of ancient lore, is a living, breathing presence in our lives today?

Living Deities: The Concept

To understand Freyja as a living deity, one must first grasp the idea of living deities. Unlike traditional religious entities which might be seen as remote or relegated to sacred scriptures, living deities permeate our existence. They evolve with us, respond to our present needs, and interact in a dynamic dance of energy, synchronicity, and guidance. Just as a river never remains the same from moment to moment, living deities don't remain frozen in age-old tales. They flow, transform, and ripple through our consciousness in unexpected ways.

The Modern Freyja: Archetypes and Symbols

Carl Jung, the Swiss psychiatrist and psychoanalyst, introduced the concept of archetypes – universal, primal symbols and images shared by humanity. These symbols resonate across time, unconfined by geography or culture. Freyja, as the Sensual Mystic, certainly fits this mold. Today, her spirit can be seen in the empowered individuals who assert their autonomy, in the passionate lovers who aren't afraid of their desires, and in those who embrace both their warrior and nurturer selves.

While we might not witness chariots driven by cats in our streets, think about the modern symbols of independence, grace, and agility. Consider how the essence of Freyja's feline companions can be spotted in the poised catwalk of a model or the agile leap of an athlete. It's not about the literal translation of myths but the symbolic resonance they hold today.

Personal Anecdotes: Freyja in Unexpected Places

I once met a woman, Lila, during a spiritual retreat in Iceland. She shared a story of a time she felt lost, her life seemingly devoid of passion or purpose. One night, she dreamt of a powerful figure, a woman radiant in golden light, surrounded by cats, and in the background, the Northern Lights danced. This figure beckoned Lila to dance. As they danced, Lila felt a surge of energy, passion, and purpose like never before. Upon waking, she was inspired to study Norse mythology and immediately identified her dream guide as Freyja. From that day, Lila felt a deep connection with the goddess, claiming that Freyja's living essence had touched her. The dream was a turning point, and Lila embarked on a journey of self-discovery, sensuality, and empowerment.

Such stories aren't unique. Around the world, many have felt an inexplicable connection with Freyja, sensing her guidance in dreams, meditations, or moments of deep introspection.

Challenging Traditional Narratives

When we hear of Freyja in old Norse tales, she often becomes a character in a narrative – beautiful, powerful, but distant. Yet, the real challenge lies in letting go of the need to see deities as fixed entities, distant from our mundane lives. By recognizing the essence of Freyja in the world around us and within ourselves, we bridge the gap between the mythical and the real.

The Dynamic Dance: Engaging with the Living Freyja

So, how does one connect with this living Freyja? The key lies not in rigorous rituals but in awareness. Begin by observing moments in your life where you felt empowered, loved, desired, or connected to a deeper wisdom. Each of these moments holds a spark of Freyja. By acknowledging her presence in such moments, you strengthen your bond with her living essence.

Meditation can serve as a powerful tool. Instead of approaching meditation with a goal to 'meet' Freyja, enter it with an open heart, allowing her energy to manifest as it chooses. It might be a feeling, a vision, or a sudden insight. Trust the process, for the living deity knows no bounds or structures.

Freyja's tales from the ancient Norse sagas are undeniably enchanting. But more magical is the idea that she is not confined to those pages or bygone eras. She is here, now, touching lives, guiding souls, and dancing in the hearts of those who dare to feel, love, and be.

To understand Freyja as a living deity is to challenge traditional narratives and to expand one's spiritual horizons. It's a call to recognize the divine not just in sacred texts but in the laughter of a loved one, in the warmth of a passionate embrace, in the courage to stand up for oneself, and in the quiet wisdom that whispers in the soul.

Beyond myths, in the living tapestry of our daily experiences, Freyja thrives. Embrace her, and you embrace a part of yourself – ancient, powerful, and eternally alive.

Chapter 20: Concluding the Journey - Eternal Connection

The quest for deeper understanding, a profound spiritual bond, and personal transformation is neither linear nor finite. It is a winding road filled with unexpected revelations, moments of doubt, and bursts of enlightenment. As we conclude our journey with the enigmatic Freyja, it's essential to look back, celebrate our milestones, and understand that while one chapter may end, another beckons.

Reflecting on the Journey with Freyja

Our expedition with Freyja has been a mosaic of experiences. From understanding her dual nature, a seamless blend of fierce warrior and sensual lover, to embracing the magic of Seidr and the allure of dreams, every step has added a new layer to our consciousness. The goddess, in her multifaceted glory, has shown us the importance of balance—strength with vulnerability, desire with discernment, and dreams with reality.

Throughout this voyage, many may have experienced personal metamorphoses. Freyja's teachings encourage transformation, not just in the spiritual realm but in the tangible world. The goddess does not advocate for blind adherence but rather introspection and personal resonance. Reflect on the moments when her teachings resonated with your personal experiences. Perhaps it was when you acknowledged your desires without judgment, danced uninhibitedly to celebrate life, or felt a surge of warrior-like strength in the face of adversity.

It's also important to acknowledge moments of uncertainty or disconnect. Spirituality, much like any other journey, is not devoid of bumps. There might have been concepts that were challenging or rituals that felt alien. And that's okay. Freyja, in all her wisdom, celebrates the quest itself, not just the milestones.

Eternal Bond – The Way Forward

The beauty of our bond with Freyja is its eternal nature. While the chapters of this guide may end, the relationship with the goddess doesn't. The Norse goddess of love, fertility, and war extends an invitation, not just to understand her lore but to intertwine our lives with hers. Here are ways to ensure that our bond with Freyja remains strong, evolving, and eternal:

Daily Devotion: Setting aside a few moments daily, whether in meditation, silent reflection, or a dedicated ritual, can keep the connection alive. Your space needn't be elaborate—a simple altar with her symbols, a candle, and perhaps some incense can suffice. It's the intent and dedication that matter most.

Embrace Nature: Freyja's essence is deeply rooted in nature. Regular walks in the woods, tending to a garden, or even moments spent admiring the moon can be seen as acts of devotion. The rustle of leaves, the gurgling of a stream, or the fragrance of night-blooming flowers can be gentle reminders of her presence.

Continuous Learning: Dive deeper into Norse mythology, explore texts that delve into Seidr magic, or perhaps embark on a study of other goddesses. The more we learn, the richer our understanding of Freyja becomes.

Community Engagement: Join or create communities that celebrate Freyja. Engaging in group rituals, discussions, or even art-based projects dedicated to the goddess can enhance your connection and understanding. It's in shared experiences and collective energy that many find profound spiritual growth.

Personal Rituals: While traditional rituals have their significance, creating personal rituals can be deeply fulfilling. It could be as simple as wearing jewelry that reminds you of her, incorporating dance into your daily routine, or setting up dream journals.

Teach and Share: Share your experiences and knowledge with others. Whether it's through writing, speaking, or art, teaching is not just a way to spread the word but also to solidify your understanding.

Our relationship with Freyja, like any other, requires nurturing, understanding, and continuous engagement. There will be moments of profound connection and times of distance. But in the heart of it all, the goddess's wisdom remains—a beacon guiding us through life's mysteries.

Freyja, in her boundless grace, does not demand unwavering faith. Instead, she celebrates the journey, the quest for knowledge, and the dance of existence. With her by our side, every step, no matter how trivial, becomes a dance of magic, sensuality, and cosmic wonder. Let's carry forward her teachings, her essence, and her blessings, making our bond with her not just a chapter but a lifelong saga of love, learning, and luminescence.

Made in United States
Troutdale, OR
12/05/2023